THE MISSING LINKS

WHERE OUR BONDS ARE BROKEN

THE MISSING LINKS
– Where Our Bonds Are Broken
Copyright © 2018 Randolph W. Mack. All rights reserved.

F I R S T   E D I T I O N
Published in 2019

Author: Randolph W. Mack

Website: www.RWMack.com

ISBN: 978-1-7337299-2-5

Library of Congress Control Number: TXu2-105-136 | July 5, 2018

Category: Family, Relationships, Social

Library of Congress Cataloging-in-Publication Data

Editor: Barbara Joe (Amani Publishing LLC)

Proofreader: Kiera J. Northington (itsthewritestuff.com)

Photographer: Eric Bennett

Cover Designer: Barbara Upshaw-Mayers (Aura Graphics and Design)

Publishing Consultant & Formatting: Eli Blyden | EliTheBookGuy.com

Printed & Published in the United States of America

DEDICATION

This book is dedicated to God, who has sustained me through all of my trials. I've come to the point in my life where I realize the things we go through, as people, are not allowed or caused by God for the purpose of our suffering, but so His glory can be seen when we emerge on the other side of whatever caused us to feel helpless.

Thank You my Lord, for I truly believe and have witnessed Your truth – that You will never leave me nor forsake me. Thank You for showing me Your light when I was engulfed in darkness. By Your light, I'm able to see beyond where I was to where You wanted me to be.

Thank You for giving me the will to fight a good fight against the temptation of giving up on life, of which there were many times.

Thank You, my Lord, for allowing me to be acceptable in Your sight and for letting me be chosen by You to understand Your will and Your way. You are truly merciful.

Thank You for my children: Yasmine, Shiloh, Adonis, and Giavonnie. I will do my best to guide them back to You, for I know they were Yours before they became mine.

Thank You for blessing me with a virtuous mother. Her example of love inspired me to not only understand compassion, it also compelled me to seek Your kingdom. Through her, I became not who I could have been, but who I am meant to be. Thank You, Lord, for revealing Yourself to me. My faith in You is unwavering. I love You with all I am. Please continue to strengthen me daily to do Your will. Please let this book become a message to some and motivation to others. Let the chapters be used as tools to build and bring families closer. But first and foremost, let the glory be Yours, so I will serve as a witness that all things are possible through You and that Your word will not return unto You void.

Let Your will be done through me.

TABLE OF CONTENTS

THE MISSING LINKS

WHERE OUR BONDS ARE BROKEN

RANDOLPH W. MACK

INTRODUCTION

This book is based on my perspective of what has divided grandparents from grandchildren, fathers from sons, mothers from daughters and in general, the causes and effects it's had on families.

The state of families today has been reduced to fragments of what they were twenty or thirty years ago. The unity, respect and leadership that were the glue to sustain families through trials are non-existent now. Some of these problems are by choice and can be easily overcome. But some are by force, which can also be overcome. However, it could take measures beyond individuals and instead a collective effort, with persistence, patience and prayer too help families to overcome all the obstacles that may stand between its unity.

The reason society is so careless, reckless and dangerous today is that to have a democracy; we have to have experienced the structure of a family first, which is the first place where we learn respect, compassion and unity. Without these values being instilled in our youth today, we are seeing a generation of kids who don't care about anything but drugs, sex and rap! If this continues to go unchecked, things are only going to become worse not only for families but also for society as a whole. Make no mistake about it; these same kids are the future. It won't make a difference if they go to college or prison—if they work at a fast food joint or become a person with a job considered prestigious. Without morals, compassion and consideration for others, one is no different than the other. This should be evident by the unparalleled number of elected officials who have been indicted for corruption in the last decade alone. Both may travel different paths, but subsequently, end up in the same place.

I truly believe in the human spirit being able to overcome adversity. With a renewed faith in our religion, regardless of whom or what that may be, I feel we can overcome any and everything as a family.

I hope this book will encourage and compel family leaders to reunify their families while leading others to evaluate their priorities and put them in perspective with strong family values. I hold this same hope for my own family that it will unify us back to the former glory we had when my mother was the matriarch.

If your family is unified, I hope something in this book can further strengthen it. If only one chapter applies, I hope a resolution is suggested or you will conclude one of your own. And if you will accept it to be true that a family that prays together stays together, then let prayer become your sunrises and faith your sunsets.

CHAPTER 1

Love and Relationships

---◇---

To be in a relationship where the feelings are mutual, the attraction intense and the level of love that's shared surpasses the physical aspect and reaches the mental, emotional and spiritual apex is indeed a beautiful thing. Even though it seems everyone has their own interpretation of what love is and should be, love is simultaneous with the truth. They each stand alone. They are indivisible and encompass the very essence of God.

Every chapter of this book can be resolved with love. The reason most of the chapters are in this book is because the subjects lack love. If love is injected back into the family, it will inspire unity, respect and maturity, which will present opportunities for someone to step up and assume the role of being a leader. A leader who not only cares about family, but loves God and lives life according to His will and way.

Today, it seems as if love has been replaced by lust, which may seem appealing. But in truth, lust does not have a good track record of longevity. This may explain why the average new relationship lasts for only three to six months and the relationships that do progress to the point of marriage, more than likely, will end up in divorce court within two years.

I can recall going to family court, which is also where divorce court is held one day in regards to getting sole custody of my sons. I noticed it was crowded, so I asked a guy standing next to me why it was so many people in the area. He replied, saying the divorce rate was higher than it's ever been and so many people file for divorce that the courts make them wait for two years before it will allow them to file. A guy next to him interjected that the courts were not making them wait two years to file, but the courts were actually two years behind on resolving divorce petitions.

This combined with the average time of relationships that don't involve marriage; it seems the relationships most people are getting involved in are based on everything but love.

One major contributing factor is that in the African American community, there seems to be a shortage of available men. It's been said, ever since I can remember, that African American women outnumber African American men. Based on numbers alone, the fact that many African Americans are in prisons and jails across America is taken into account with the number of faithfully married men, gay men, ones in interracial relationships and the ones mature women would not consider on their level, the number of eligible men could be reaching the point of extinction.

There's an old saying that desperate times call for desperate measures. This seems to be what's driving a lot of women to lower their standards for the sake of being with someone. The reason I said women and did not include men is because men today know how the ratio is between women and us. So a lot of men have taken the position that they can have their cake and eat it too. Some have multiple women at one time, and some change women like they're changing clothes.

I understand how women want to be loved and be in love, how depressing it can be to be lonely and alone, and even how a broken relationship can cause some to question their self-worth. But ladies, let me tell you. I also know how it looks and feels to see a loved one die slowly from a preventable disease. I watched Patricia Green go from being a virtuous woman in the prime of her life to looking as if she'd aged fifty years in five. Patricia didn't smoke, drink or go out, period. She was married to Sam, a man she loved and lived for and was also faithful to him, for over twenty years. Patricia was an unwavering believer in God, whose sunrises began with prayer and sunsets ended with faith. Patricia was the matriarch of her family and an inspiration to her friends. She was a leader, who led by example and embraced before she criticized. I'm speaking of Patricia in the past tense because she's deceased. Sam, the man she loved so much, is the same man who brought death into their home. He cheated on her and contracted the virus known as Human Immunodeficiency Virus or HIV and in the process, exposed her to the virus. He went on to develop full-blown Acquired Immune Deficiency Syndrome or AIDS, as a result of not taking his prescribed medication. He did this after meeting a man on the internet who told him he had a cure for HIV, but he needed to stop taking his medication for it to work. All the man wanted in return, was for Sam to endorse the product by declaring it eliminated the virus from his system. At this point, Sam was desperate and would have tried anything to be cured, rather than trying to manage the disease through medication. He stopped taking his medication after having been fully informed about the risks and that the results of doing so, could cause his HIV to develop into full-blown AIDS. When Sam decided to do so, it gave credence to the old saying that desperate times call for desperate measures.

Once his status changed from HIV positive to full-blown AIDS, the disease decimated his body. I witnessed one of the most deadly diseases known to man tear him apart, piece by piece. Death soon came for him and when it did, it left Patricia to deal with her own illness, while becoming a widow. Patricia went on to live years after Sam passed away, but she suddenly died from a diabetic reaction. The thing that amazed me about Patricia was how she lived up to her marriage vows that said for better or worse, through sickness and health, for richer or poorer, 'til death do them part. She truly lived by those vows in life and even death. When Sam passed, she wore his wedding ring on her necklace until she passed. When she died, she was buried right beside him.

I know what happened to these people and the circumstances of how they came to be that way because the lady I'm speaking of was my friend, my confidante, my teacher, my spiritual advisor, who never questioned God or His will. To me, she was the epitome of a woman; this lady was also my mother.

And to those reading this book, the moral of the story is if something does not work, ignoring it will not fix it. You don't have to stick your hands in the fire to know it will burn you. Pay attention to the signs, rather than how you're going to pay a bill, because there are no bills in the graveyard. Being married and being happily married are two different things.

I'm sure my mom is not the first person to experience what she did and I'm certain she won't be the last. So, as I said earlier, I can sympathize with people not wanting to be alone or lonely. I too wish I could find the missing piece of my life's puzzle that when joined with me, would complete the total picture of love. But not to the point where I would put my life at risk to be with someone who doesn't care about her own life.

Imagine being lonely and then imagine being alone and dying. Because if we have the misfortune of being exposed to one of the deadly diseases going around, the person who gave it to us, more than likely won't be anywhere around us. The difference is now we're lonely. Slip up, and we will be lonely and dying. Or for that matter, someone else can slip up and put us face-to-face with death.

As I've written in this chapter, it seems everyone has their own interpretation of love and what it does and doesn't do. But, the best definition I've ever come across was in the Bible in the book of Corinthians, Chapter 1:4-7 that says, "Love is patient; love is kind. It does not envy; it does not boast; it is not proud. It is not rude; it is not self-seeking; it is not easily angered; it keeps no record of wrongs. Love does not delight in evil, but rejoices with the truth. It always protects, always trusts, always hopes, and always perseveres." If these principles and standards were met and not exceeded, were applied to our relationships and families, the problems too many people are faced with would be alleviated, especially the mistake some make of equating sex with love.

I've heard many people say their own expectations were being met. But to ensure the relationship will last, it's imperative one not only be in love but make sure it's love and not simply lust. I want to direct this next statement to the women who have children from men not involved in their lives or their child's life for whatever reason.

However you may feel about the father now, if it's not positive, maybe it's best you keep that to yourself. The reason I say that is because, have you ever thought about how the children may look at you when you are constantly criticizing their father by saying he's no good and how much you dislike him? Whether you realize it or not, you have to know the child will formulate the question of why did you get pregnant from someone you have no respect for? Not only that, they may question how you can unconditionally love them if you hate their fathers, whom they are half of, without having any resentment toward them?

This reminds me of the saying that when you point a finger at someone, three are pointing back at you. This is especially true of women who may have been wide open when they got pregnant, then eventually matured and got their priorities in perspective to become a good parent. It seems since they got themselves together, everybody else is messed up. When in truth, they were more irresponsible than the man was by not protecting themselves from an unplanned pregnancy or possibly a deadly disease. I would think in this day and age that if consenting adults agree to be intimate, they would at least use protection. Casual sex is not only dangerous if unprotected, but it's also a clear sign those doing it have no self-respect or regard for their lives.

Let me sum it up like this: there's a difference between love and lust. Use the standards from Corinthians 13:4-7 as a measure to identify true love. Remember the excitement of a sexual relationship is only for the moment; death is forever and desire should not deceive someone into desperation.

CHAPTER 2

The Love of Money

◇

Timothy 6:9-10 says, "People who want to get rich fall into temptation and a trap and into many foolish and harmful desires that plunge men into ruin and destruction. For the love of money is the root of all evil. Some people, eager for money, have wandered from the faith and pierced themselves with many griefs."

Ecclesiastes 5:10 says, "Whoever loves money never has enough; whoever loves wealth is never satisfied with his income."

Proverbs 11:4 says, "Wealth is worthless in the day of wrath, but righteousness delivers from death."

Proverbs 11:28 says, "Whoever trusts in his riches will fall, but the righteous will thrive like a green leaf."

Matthew 6:19 says, "Do not store up for yourselves treasures on earth, where moth and rust destroy and where thieves break in and steal, but store up for yourselves treasures in heaven, where moth and rust do not destroy and where thieves do not break in and steal. For where your treasure is, there your heart will be also."

Matthew 19:23-24 says, "Then Jesus said to his disciples, 'I tell you the truth, it is harder for a rich man to enter the kingdom of heaven. Again I tell you, it is easier for a camel to go through the eye of a needle than for a rich man to enter rude kingdom of God.'"

I started this chapter off this way to give God's point-of-view on riches. Many people are in love with their wealth and possessions, think of nothing other than getting money and are willing to sacrifice so much to get it and keep it until they will trade heaven for hell to do so. Before I go on, let's be clear on one point: God does not say that money is the root of all evil. He says the "love" of money is the root of all evil.

All children see today is people promoting fame and fortune. It's creating a generation of kids only wanting to wear designer clothes and shoes, jewelry with diamonds and they all want expensive cars. These kids are even exposed to this at young ages by their mothers or parents buying them Jordan tennis shoes and only clothes with the name of some designer on them. I have done this with my kids also; all parents want their kids to have the best. I think it's also important for their self-esteem and allows them to fit in with their peers.

The downside to bringing these kids up like this is that it has created a materialistic generation expecting these things. As they get older, nothing seems to be acceptable to them if it's not name brand. For a lot of these kids, when they become teenagers and start trying to establish independence, they quickly get a rude awakening upon realizing how expensive everything is, especially when all the things they want cost a lot of money. This is the point where a lot of young boys start engaging in crime so they can get the material things. This is also the time when some young ladies become willing to get involved in relationships that expose them to the finer things in life, material things.

These kids are seeing fame and fortune being promoted in everything they see on television, if not it's promoting sex or violence. The music industry is probably the biggest promoter of material things, riches, sexual promiscuity and drinking alcohol. Because of the greed and love of money the music executives have, they don't care about the negative influence and effect it's having on these kids. Almost every rap video is filled with girls dancing around, while guys sing about how they have all the women. The young guys want to emulate the rappers with all the girls in the videos. A lot of girls want to emulate the women in these videos. Some of the young girls see the way women dance in music videos and how it's glamorized, and want to become strippers. When they see beautiful women doing it, they think it's okay and the boys and girls being affected by this don't realize these people are entertainers. Lil Wayne and TI sing about being gangsters. But when they get arrested, they get one year in prison, while the kids that try to be like them end up with a hundred years for doing the same thing.

Something else that's misleading a lot of kids is the prospect of becoming a professional athlete and earning a hundred-million-dollar contract. Every parent with a child playing little league sports, all the way to high school and even college, think their child is the next superstar in the making. In truth, every professional sport in America combined does not have 5,000 athletes. That's including baseball, football, basketball, hockey, tennis, and soccer. As parents, we should encourage our children to pursue higher learning because although it's only a few thousand professional sports positions and even less in music and entertainment, there are tens of thousands of CEO, COO and CFO jobs, not just in America but abroad. We need to enrich our children with culture, character, morals, principals, values, self-esteem and virtue. These are the qualities that will give them the essentials to make it once they are on their own.

If we, as the gatekeepers for this generation, do not start to lead these children, they will continue to follow the belief that if it doesn't make dollars, it doesn't make sense. It's not just children obsessed with becoming rich that's causing them to be willing to go to any extreme to get it. It's politicians, preachers, lawyers, doctors and even teachers. For a lot of people, it doesn't matter if it's by hook or by crook; it's all about the Benjamin's.

We must restore the bonds of need that have been broken by greed. Character will get us in places that cash won't! Like the Scriptures say, "The love of money is the root of all evil." I firmly believe that's the same reason most of these bonds were broken.

CHAPTER 3

Maturity

Maturity is defined as being fully developed in body and mind. I included maturity as being one of the missing links because of the way some adults are today. One of the most backward things I've ever heard is when people say forty is the new thirty, or thirty is the new twenty. I guess that means if you're twenty, you're the new ten-year-old. Maybe that explains (for men at least) why we have some twenty, thirty, forty and even fifty-year-olds more into playing video games than being with their children.

The first place kids are taught is at home. If the parents have no leadership skills, then despite having teachers at school, they will follow the examples they see on television or whatever environment they are exposed to by peers. Teachers teach kids about different subjects relating to school. Parents teach kids about right from wrong, respect, manners and values. This is how it should be. But today, children are being awakened between 5:30 – 6 a.m. to be taken to daycare or school and some have to be up to catch the bus. By the time school is over, it's 2 or 3 p.m. Some kids go to afterschool programs, and some are in daycare until 5 or 6 p.m., when their parents get off work. The older ones are home or hanging out until their parents get home after work. Considering rush hour traffic, these kids are not getting home until between 6 and 7 p.m. and the older ones don't see their parents until this time also.

By the time parents get home, take a shower and eat dinner, it's time for them to go to sleep to be rested for the next day. Once we look at it this way we realize that at the most we are interacting with our children for one hour in the morning and three hours after school, before they go back to sleep. This means they are with someone else or somewhere else for up to twelve hours a day. We as adults need to make sure we are attentive to our children more than we are to our video games. The same principles apply to the young ladies pursuing a relationship and want to keep the kids as invisible as possible, thinking it will keep the man or "boy" wanting to stay.

As a man, I can tell any female it's a turn-on to be desired by a woman. But, at the same time I want to say it's a turn-off to be involved with a desperate female. When I say desperate, I mean a female who seems like she can meet a man and be willing to do anything and everything to keep him. She doesn't know anything about his medical background, his reason for being available for her to date, or even if he has a criminal history. All that seems to matter is if he has a penis.

When I speak of maturity, I'm also speaking about how we must be parents and teachers to our children before we are friends. Yes, having a friendship with our children is important, but not the kind that involves smoking weed with them, going out to clubs with them, borrowing their Lil Wayne or Jay Z CDs, or dating friends either too old for the daughter, or too young for the mother. I directed the dating aspect to women, because men rarely have these types of interactions with their fathers. I don't want to appear critical toward women. Truth is, women are the head of the household in most families today. They are the leaders; they are the ones taking care of birthdays being acknowledged, school being attended, providing food and substantially more and more are the only ones taking kids to their sports practice.

When women can work and play the role of both parents, they should be commended. When we see women with their daughters and we can't tell which one is the parent, or we see them with their sons and she's dressed in a way that we can't tell if she's his parent or girlfriend, these are the ones misleading our youth and need to be checked.

One problem is we are in a generation where we see women becoming great grandmothers at forty-five years old. Some females have children at young ages, such as fourteen and fifteen years old. By the time she turns thirty, her child is now pregnant at fifteen, which makes her a grandmother at thirty and her mother a great grandmother at forty-five. This is a vicious cycle being repeated in this generation. Some of these great grandmothers and grandmothers refuse to accept they are such. They go out with their children to bars, dress and act like the grandchildren, even listening and dancing to the same music. There are great grandmothers dating guys young enough for their great grandchild. It's a common sight to see three generations of a family of females out together, and the older one is acting like she is the youngest.

This cycle has to be broken; it's like the blind leading the blind. How can we show someone the way if we can't see it ourselves?

The same changes need to be made with the men today. They need to grow up and stop putting video games before their families. Some of these so-called men will raise hell if their kids even go near their games and will go completely off on their kids' mothers for letting them go near the games.

I agree everyone should take time out to relax and do something entertaining and even stimulating. But if going out to clubs is still your favorite pastime at thirty or older and you've been doing it since you were twenty, you need to grow your life and expand your activities to include things more in perspective with your age. For example, take a cruise, take the kids to Disney World, go see other states; in other words, get some culture. Do some grown-up things with your spouse and kids; lead by example and inspire your kids to look up to you. In essence, while you are growing, your family will grow with you.

Another thing a lot of us need to mature about is how to stop thinking it's all about getting high and getting by. We should be focused on staying fed and getting ahead. When we were young, some of us experimented with getting high with different drugs and drinks. For some, it never went past occasional weed and drinking. Today, so many people have taken getting a buzz to another level that now involves weed, pills, cocaine, and drinking. It is a clear sign of immaturity and a lack of self-control when we feel normal or good from having so many things in our bodies and thinking we are truly at our best when we're on all those drugs. Realize how much money is spent a day on it, then multiply it by thirty to represent a month. Just getting twenty dollars of weed a day, or a combination of drugs each day for thirty days, is six hundred dollars a month. When I say a combination of drugs, it could be ten dollars on cigarettes and blunts, ten on weed or pills, and five on drinks is twenty-five dollars a day. But I, as well as all of the people doing this, know it's more than this a day. And on the days it's not, we will somehow make it still average out to the same amount by getting more on some days than others. I consider this immature because if we make fifteen or sixteen hundred a month and we spend six or seven hundred a month getting high, then it's clear we have not fully matured.

Another sign of immaturity in males today is in the way some of us dress. I have seen a lot of fashions and trends come and go in my generation. Nothing comes close to the way I now see grown men walking around with their pants hanging low and their underwear showing. How can someone feel like they are acting like an adult while dressing like a child? It's not acceptable anywhere outside of the city, or in any business type setting. Nor is it acceptable at their own relatives' houses. When I see men dressed like this, my impression is they have no intention of going outside the small circle they live in. They want to be perceived as thugs or men who give less than a damn what people think of them. This is the image they want to project. The bad part about it is if they have a son or sons, they see this and in their minds, they feel it's cool because they see their own fathers doing it. If the sons have bonded with their fathers, they look up to them and want to be like their dads. To some fathers, it may be cool to see their little man act this way while they are kids trying to be tough. The drawback is when they grow into this mentality and not only like it, they become it.

CHAPTER 4

Respect

Respect, in some of our youth today, seems to be gained from how much disrespect they put out. The more they cuss, wear their pants hanging low, don't go to school, get in trouble with the law and act grown the more respect they seem to get.

These kids nowadays don't respect Dr. Martin Luther King Jr.'s vision or his dream. They don't respect the adversities that were surpassed by the leaders of the civil rights movement nor the people themselves. They don't care about family; they are more loyal to their partners in crime than their families. They don't care about their neighbors. A lot of them don't even give a damn about themselves. It's sad, but it's true. A lot of them don't care about God, or if they go to heaven or hell because to them, they are already experiencing one or the other right here on earth.

So much was sacrificed for us to be where we are today. This is particularly true of African Americans. The lives that were taken and some willingly given were done so not for their own benefit but rather to secure a place in the future for the ones coming after them.

Some people gave their lives so they would not be called niggers. If they could see the lack of appreciation this generation has for what these people gave up, especially the way the word nigger is used to refer to each other, they would probably consider it more disrespectful than the people who used it to degrade us and treat us with less respect than was given to animals.

When I spoke of sacrificed lives, it was not only to be treated as human beings; it was also for the right to vote, sit on a bus, to attend school, to play sports and be able to sit in a restaurant to eat.

The whole purpose of the resistance was for respect. There were no requests for it. There was a demand that they would be treated as equals. Not equals to them but equal in opportunities, love, life, health, and wealth.

Now how can we, as people, not respect the doors that were opened for us with these people's lives, blood, sweat and tears? How can we call each other the very names they died for us not to be called? How can we not respect them when they wanted respect for us before we were even born?

Beyond their sacrifices was the one made by God. He gave His only begotten Son to save us. Whether we believe in this or any other religion, can we say this higher power we believe in is respected by people today? There are more scandals today in the church than in politics.

A lot of the youth don't respect God because they don't have faith or even a belief that He's real. In turn, they justify not believing based on the excuse they don't know God.

My point is it seems the lack of respect has spread beyond society and reached the most sacred relationships we are a part of. This includes our faith in God, unity within our families and even marriages. The divorce rate is higher now than ever before in history and the average relationship only lasts three to six months. Men are disrespecting women more with domestic violence and infidelity being committed by both sexes has led us to the state we're in today, which is no respect for ourselves.

I included respect as one of the missing links in this book because with respect comes consideration about the things we do and how it will affect others. With respect comes peace that would also bring harmony to our families, relationships, society and even the world. With respect comes care, unity and even democracy. However, democracy cannot be attained if the first place we learn to respect the rights and wishes of others have now become the place where we learn malice, which is at home.

I often wonder, is it possible to get back to where we once were as families and society regarding respect? I know it's not impossible because it's simply a matter of choosing to give it to receive it. The question though, is will people collectively want to?

Have we let our youth get so far from us that we can't reconcile the differences that have come between us? If all they have to pass on to the next generation is what they value now, what will be gained as they pass on that which sustains them?

The pace most of our youth are traveling on the roads today could lead to a dead-end. It's possible they could even self-destruct. With jail and prison replacing school, the numerous deadly diseases and the extreme violence these kids and young adults are facing, the prospects of survival seem limited if not grim.

Do we, as the parents, leaders and gatekeepers of these children sit back and watch what's going on saying these kids are too dangerous to try to change? Rather than trying to redirect their destinies, we become the generation that didn't have the resolve, to keep our lineage going by overcoming the trials and tribulations we are faced with the same way those before us did. Considering the challenges they faced back then in comparison to the ones we need to deal with today, we should be able to reignite the flame of respect that got us through some of the darkest nights any group of people on earth has ever dealt with.

The same flame of respect can illuminate compassion within us and inspire us to save our youth. We must approach this objective with respect for them being our children, grandchildren and our people; the same people who Martin fought to liberate and the same people God gave His Son to save. If this is not a part of our belief, as far as what we believe in regarding religion, couldn't we agree what or whoever we believe in would be pleased to see us trying to save this generation?

I firmly believe that when we lost respect for each other, as people, the doors were opened for violence, wars, murders and the destruction of families and society as a whole.

I also firmly believe if we regroup and build on what's right with our youth and encourage them, inspire them and embrace them rather than focusing on their wrongs and pointing fingers, these kids can reach their potential instead of a prison or worse, a cemetery.

In essence, it will take unity!

CHAPTER 5

Unity

U nity is defined as being in the state of oneness. Unity, along with respect, became the driving force behind the Civil Rights Movement. Without these two, the rights afforded to us today would not exist. Considering the challenges those of the movement faced such as being attacked by dogs, being sprayed with high powered water hoses, being tormented by the KKK, and even killed with bombs, the unity had to be one unparalleled to this day.

Speaking of civil rights, it was not something pursued by only blacks. White women, as well as other minorities, joined the push toward equality. So the level of unity surpassed racial boundaries and unified the most unlikely of people to accomplish the goal of respect.

Unity helped us overcome some of the most hostile oppressions known to man, all to reach the goal of respect. If we can humble ourselves to reach out to each other, I believe the same unity that helped us overcome back then, can inspire us and unify us today to the point of having respect again for our neighbors, families, children, parents, loved ones and even God.

For this to happen there must be an envisioned goal as far as what the purpose or cause would be. If one needs to be suggested, how about for peace? That alone is enough. But if more is needed, the purpose of saving our youth from self-destruction and simply because it's the right thing to do are more than enough. Being selfish and thinking of only going to work and coming back home and locking ourselves in our homes, cutting ourselves off from the world is not going to make us safer. Or seeing the news daily and seeing other people become victims of crime or violence and assuming it always happens to other people—not realizing that was probably the same thing they were watching and thinking the day before or even the same day.

No one is safe anywhere today from the violence and disregard people have for each other. If this problem is not confronted now, tomorrow may be too late.

When I was young, I lived in the Central Park Projects in Tampa, Florida. They were in a rough and tough section of town. While the environment was limited, the unity was as if we were all one family. If one of the parents saw a kid acting up, the parent not only confronted the child about it but took it a step further and gave out a whipping. Then that parent would tell the kid to go tell his or her mom what happened and why.

It was best to go tell our parents because if we didn't, by the time the neighbor told it and we had not already, we might get it again from the neighbor for not doing as we were told. And then get it again from our moms for whatever it was we did in the first place.

Today, in the same situation, no one will say anything to these children if they see them doing something wrong. These children will cuss us out, threaten us and even kill us if we offend them. When our elders see youngsters today, they try not to even make eye contact. Can't we tell how bad it's gotten when we see a group of young men coming toward us, regardless of where we are going, and instant fear strikes us? The first thing we think is danger! This does not have to be somewhere in public. There can be two or three or even just one teenager coming to our home asking if we want our grass cut and we will swear it's some kind of set-up.

There used to be a time when adults could hear us cussing with a group of friends, and they would talk to us and make us feel bad and it would cause us to apologize. Now people can see us being robbed, beaten, raped, or even killed and the most they will do is record it with their phones. But if our life depended on them intervening, we would probably be in a world of trouble.

The bottom line is that without respect, we cannot expect unity. And without unity, we can expect the destruction of families, communities and the world to accelerate. Unity is one of the components that cannot be excluded from the overall elements that are essential in maintaining democracy, families and society.

Unity is the first thing we must pursue to restore links that have been broken to accomplish anything, including restoration of our families, respect of our fellow man and even world peace. If unity is not the first thing we pursue, how can anything be agreed upon?

As I write this chapter, I find myself facing the question of would I be willing to put forth the effort to help try to restore the unity I experienced growing up by reaching out to some of the youth today? Without hesitation, the answer is yes. I believe a lot of people have tried to do so. The problem is these kids can relate to the message they bring because the truth makes sense and stands alone to everyone. They just can't relate to the people who are the messengers.

I feel they can relate to me and the message. Sometimes it takes a man to humble a boy. What I mean is we cannot be afraid of these kids because they can smell fear a mile away. Their lack of respect must be matched with the spirit of determination that helped our elders go forward even when faced with the prospect of death.

These are not bad kids; they are just doing some bad things. If I had to give one answer as to why I think these kids, especially the young men, are the way they are, I would say they don't have their fathers in their lives. Fathers are one of the most vital links that must be restored to bridge the gap that has grown between us and our youth today.

CHAPTER 6

Fathers

———◆———

Included fathers as one of the missing links in this book, because the absence of so many fathers is one of the main reasons a lot of young men are acting the way they are. The mothers of today are playing the roles of both mother and father to their children and should be commended for the way they provide guidance, shelter, safety, comfort and for the way they are supporting their kids in sports. However, the fact remains that a boy should have a man's influence in his life. This is not to say that some young men raised by their mothers alone have not turned out to be good kids, but they are the exception not the rule.

There are many things preventing fathers from being a part of their kids' lives. One major cause is their fathers are incarcerated, especially in the African American community. America has more people in prison than any other country in the world. At present, there are over 1.5 million men and women in prisons in America. That's not including the hundreds of thousands in county jails.

As I said, I believed it was a conspiracy until I accepted that if we don't commit crimes, there will be no reasons to arrest us. We can't break the laws and then say it's a conspiracy, especially when we know how minorities are being treated in the justice system. The Bible says in Proverbs that even if a bird sees you laying a trap, it will not fly into it.

So if we know it's a trap, why would we commit the crimes that are getting a lot of people life sentences?

Another big problem is a lot of children were conceived from one-night stands and casual relationships not involving any commitment. A lot of people having children don't know anything about each other except their names and sometimes it's just their nicknames. They don't know each other's medical history, family members, or any other vital information about each other.

This eventually leads to child support, which is worse than being on parole. Imagine being contacted by a court telling you to appear on the issue of child support when you as a man, didn't even know you had a child. The first thing you do is try to figure out who this is saying you have a child by her, because you see her real name being used as the petitioner (the one who is accusing you) when you only know her by her nickname of Candy, Cookie, Shortie, or something.

Once you show up for court, you're told you have a child and you are two or three years behind on payments, which gives you one account. You're told you have an ongoing account you are expected to pay monthly. So now, you have two accounts. Then you're told for the two years you didn't pay, (Cookie or Candy) was receiving Aid to Families with Dependent Children or AFDC, and that gives you a third account. So you've got three accounts you have to start paying on. You may have settled down and even gotten married; now the majority of your income will be going to someone for a child you have never even seen. Not only that, you are told your driver's license could be suspended until you get caught up on your payments.

This will not only put a strain on your relationship or marriage, but could destroy it. It will cause you to look at the child as child support rather than as your child. The prospect of paying child support can be so stressful until some men don't even want to see their children. Sometimes it's to convince their current spouses there's no connection between them and the child's mother and it won't be anything renewed between them. Another reason is that some men consider these women as nothing more than someone they slept with in passing and they have no respect for them and now they have to pay them for the next eighteen years.

The bad part about this is it brings division between the father and child. I agree that men and women should help contribute to the support of their children. But let's evaluate if putting a person on child support is the answer. Maybe joint custody should be explored before payments. That way, support is given as well as the potential to establish a real relationship that is worth more than money. One reason would be because it gives a sense of belonging and acceptance to the kid. It also gives a kid other resources and access to the other parent's family.

Men being involved in their sons' lives can teach them the simple things like cutting grass, putting gas in cars, dressing properly, shaving faces, respecting women, respecting themselves and so many other little things adding up to big things. One of the most overlooked things fathers give their sons is a healthy sense of fear. Boys raised by their fathers may not be afraid of anything or anyone. But I guarantee you; they will be humble to their fathers.

I suggest every woman with a son try to encourage a relationship with his father. Put away the childish malice because the man has moved on and may be taking care of his other children or his stepchildren. Some women may have resentment because they feel the man has not helped with their child and assuming because of that, he doesn't care about the child she loves dearly. So her mission is not necessarily to get support but revenge.

To the ladies reading this, I can tell you from experience and observing life, you can tell these kids today their fathers did not care about them, they did not do anything for them and they are no good. But as soon as the child gets old enough to walk, run, catch a bus, ride a bike, a train, or even a plane, they will not stop until they find their fathers. And when they do, it won't be about money. It will be about love and acceptance. As long as they get that, none of the stuff you've said will matter. He may even turn against you, believing it was you who kept him from his dad.

Some ladies will say they moved on with their lives and are involved in relationships and the men in their lives have been role models for her sons. This may be true, but it's like comparing a hamburger to a steak. What I mean is, a stepfather can step in and take up the space of a father, but he still cannot take the place of their true father.

I want to be clear when I say fathers; I mean fathers, not baby daddies! Baby daddies are the ones buying one pair of tennis shoes a year and swearing they have done something. They're the ones seeing their sons with pants hanging low and thinking that's cool, teaching them how to cuss, getting high in front of them and disrespecting the children's mothers right in front of them. I'm talking about these dudes not working because they don't want to pay child support. All they want to do is hustle to get high and get by. Some of these dudes can see their sons and see the boys look just like them and they won't even acknowledge them. These are the same ones that as soon as they get locked up, they holler about who they baby mama is and who they got children with.

Another problem that can be avoided by women is choosing not to chance getting pregnant by a man she is not planning a future with; especially if she knows he has a girlfriend or a wife. It should not take having five children from five different men to realize that you've taken a wrong turn and will end up on a dead-end street.

All in all, every young man should have some influence from a man in his life. If men today don't start taking their sons under their wings the way our grandfathers did with their sons, our race will eventually become stagnant because all minorities between twenty and fifty will be locked up during the reproducing ages that should be replenishing our race. One way to get back on track is to get back in touch with our families, which is the foundation all of our ancestors stood on to see past where they were to see what was to come.

CHAPTER 7

Families-Grandparents

———◇———

I could have easily started this book on the subject of families being one of the most important factors missing from the ties essential for unity and peace. The strength of families can help overcome the most adverse situation, while at the same time, giving structure to its members as individuals and as a whole. Being a part of a strong family creates strong people. It also invokes a sense of responsibility to respect each other and one's self.

I've noticed families that have some females who are drug-free, working with dignity, pride and direction and the younger females of their families will follow their lead most of the time. I've also seen the adverse effect of young ladies from loose-knit families without a matriarch end up having kids at a young age from different boys, dropping out of school, using drugs, being in bars every weekend, and in general, their whole purpose is to get high and get by. That's not saying it's a rule but rather a routine.

This is also apparent with the young men of today. The ones coming from families with strong-willed, hardworking, settled down men tend to lead the younger men in their families in that same direction. On the other hand, the boys coming from a family where all the men are or have been locked up, use drugs and have children from multiple women seem to follow the same paths as those men.

When I speak of families, I'm talking about the ones involving a mother and father, even if they were not in a relationship or marriage, but both were still involved in their child's life. Also, grandparents if living, aunts, uncles, cousins, brothers, and sisters who are all close to each other and love and respect each other.

I've heard it said that it takes a village to raise a child. I believe this to be true and the primary teachers are the direct family members. As I've stated, while growing up in the projects the level of unity was to the extent that everyone looked out for each other's children. When I said everyone this included brothers, uncles, fathers and grandfathers. What I mean by this is that we had men in our lives. We grew up with our grandfathers teaching us about using tools, how to bait a fishing line, how to dress for church, teaching us manners and respect. This was all it took for us to have reverence for them because we knew we were loved and cherished.

One of the things that solidified my relationship with my grandfather was church. He, as well as my grandmother, was very involved in the church. My grandfather took pride in me being dressed in my Sunday best with a fresh haircut, walking in church with him. Our routine was Sunday school, church, go by KFC, pick up my grandmother's favorite meal, go to their home, and then my granddad, my brother and I watched wrestling, the same one that is now the World Wrestling Entertainment, or WWE.

I couldn't wait for Sundays to be with my granddad. The thing that excited me most was when he sat me in the driver's seat and let me drive with him while my brother and sisters were in the car heading to their home. For those moments in time, I felt like the most special kid in the world. Everyone knew I was my grandfather's, who we affectionately called Papa favorite. These were the times when grandparents were consistently involved with their grandkids. They checked report cards, held Easter egg hunts and made sure everyone had Easter baskets. More than that, they made sure we had new clothes for church as well as an outfit for after church. Christmas was something they looked forward to more than we did. They always made sure there were wrapped gifts and a tree to put them under. Birthdays always came with the guarantee of ice cream, cake and a present. My grandparents were also involved in our lives when we strayed away from the straight and narrow path. They rewarded us for doing good, but they also consistently corrected us when we needed it.

I don't know completely what has the grandparents the way they are today. I think it's two things that are the main reasons. One is they equate being involved with their grandkids with money. It's like they think every time they see their grandkids, they are going to have to buy them one thing or another and a lot of grandparents are retired and on a fixed income. Although some are still working jobs, they are on such a tight budget where every dollar count. They don't want the expectation of them doing anything placed on them, so they don't get involved the way they used to. Back then, grandparents did not necessarily make more money. The problem now is they have more expenses and the cost of living has risen. The bottom line is they can't afford to be in their grandkids lives the way their grandparents were involved in their lives.

Another reason grandparents are not involved with their grandchildren is because of their relationships with their own children. Women today don't have the same type of relationships with their mothers the way they used to have. The closeness may have been lost because of the mother trying to prevent her daughter from getting pregnant, which of course, she will then try to do.

Now the mom is sitting back saying I told you so when the same guy you got pregnant from and disrespected her for is nowhere to be found. The first thing you come to her for is to help take care of the baby. The daughter may even have children from multiple guys, and she wants her mom to watch them while she goes out to meet someone new.

Some of these grandparents feel like their kids have just left home as adults and before they can get their scent out of the house, they are back with an army of children and asking parents to watch them while they do whatever.

Another issue a grandparent has to deal with is their daughter may be only thirty and her child that's fifteen has a child which would make them great grandmothers. They may only be forty-five, as I mentioned in the chapter on maturity.

The problem with the men today is they're not the glue to keeping their families together. Most of them are not around a lot and are immature boys despite their ages. This generation doesn't value relationships with their grandparents because they are too real in their own minds and their grandparents are too square to understand them. Some guys will avoid their grandparents simply because they think they will be asked to go to church. But it's funny the way they want the grandparents to pray for them when they get in trouble.

I don't know what it is, but two women can meet each other and say nothing more than hello and hate each other. For example, if a guy takes his child's mother around his family, or even if she's just his girlfriend and they have no children—if the female does not present herself right or if she is not received right, it's a wrap. I've observed in life that once a woman forms an opinion toward another woman, it will more than likely stay that way if it's a bad opinion. And nothing, not even a grandchild, will change bad blood between two women. And if the guy is whipped enough, he will cut his mom off because she doesn't like his girlfriend or wife.

One other thing that keeps families from embracing the young men and women, even in their own families, is that these kids are pure mean and some are dangerous. I don't know what was in these kids' milk, but they are all big and look way older than they are. The thirteen- and fourteen-year-old girls look twenty and have bodies like they are twenty-five. The boys are wearing size twelve shoes by the time they are twelve. They have more hair on their face by fourteen and fifteen than their fathers.

All in all, restoring the bonds of our families will take effort, courage, determination, unity, desire, leadership, maturity, forgiveness, respect, pride, dignity and above all, love. With the restoration of families, most of the missing links will become apparent and correct themselves as the family strengthens itself.

I truly believe if families reunite, society will become unified, safer and more respectful of citizens. As I've said, for it to be a democracy, there must first be order, respect and unity at home in our families. The first step toward this goal is for someone in the family to assume the role of being the leader. It will have to be someone who will command respect as well as give it; someone who will have compassion and be firm; it will take someone strong in spirit but humble; someone with understanding and reasoning. Above all, it will have to be someone who will lead by example.

CHAPTER 8

Leadership

———◆———

With the conflicts, chaos and confusion amongst families today, it will take an exceptional person within our community, as well as in our homes, to lead us back to the roads of peace and prosperity. In the family, a mature male or female will have to assume the role of patriarch or matriarch. I don't think it's ever been a time in history when the destruction of families has been so apparent in this country. There has been injustice, wars and recessions, but all those served as reasons to become more unified as a family and society.

If asked my opinion, as to what I think is the main causes of the deterioration of families, I would say it's several factors. Some of the most obvious being absent grandparents and fathers, the age at which some youth have children and the cost of living has created a mentality of every man for himself and regardless if it's accepted as being true, prisons!

Someone, who will be able to transcend the division of party lines and prepare a table of reasoning before friends and foes, needs to emerge as a leader in the field of politics. The table should seat those with the power to persuade and the principles to pursue righteousness. A table where the courses will be unity, restructuring the family, alternatives to prison as well as restoring hope in our youth. Without these changes, this country will continue to implode. It won't be foreign terrorism, but rather acts of domestic terrorism, causing America's demise.

If unity is not restored how can we, as a society, have democracy? Without democracy, how can we have equality? Without equality, how can we have respect? Without respect, rights will be ignored. To get back to that point for African Americans would be a mockery. All these things: rights, equality, respect and democracy are interchangeable, and all demand unity.

The restoration of families is also vital. Not long ago, there were three classes of families in America: upper, middle and lower class. Now there seems to be only two, upper and lower. Middle-class America is where the most damage was done with the last recession. Middle-class America was also the largest class. With most of them losing their homes and savings, this in turn reduced them to lower class, which is another primary reason the structure of families has deteriorated so rapidly. While middle-class America was lowered to the status of lower class, simply based on income the lower class seems to have been pushed even lower. Middle-class America consisted of millions of educated people, with degrees in various sectors, who are now downplaying their credentials so they won't be overqualified for the jobs they now have to seek because of massive layoffs. A lot of the jobs they are now trying to get are the ones that were filled by the so-called lower class. Growing up, I remember adults would always say, "One day, you're going to need a college degree to work at McDonald's." It seems that day is here.

Alternatives to prison must also be addressed by the leaders trying to guide us back to a unified family and functioning democracy. Currently, there is more money being spent on corrections than the furtherance of education. While I was attending school, it was always taught that education was a deterrent to crime. Now it seems like the lawmakers are more inclined to spend more money on prisons than education. It should be apparent this approach is not working because there are more people in prisons in America than any other industrialized country in the world. Yet, the crime rate has continued to climb.

It's well documented that alternatives to prisons are more cost effective and also reduces recidivism. However, despite statistics, money is being drained from education to go to corrections. While this is being done, the cost of college tuition is increasing. So money is not only being diverted from education, but it also costs more to pursue higher education. This is like burning a candle from both ends.

What must not be overlooked is the effect prisons are having on families. Possibly 95 percent of prisoners are adults. A large percentage of them have children who know where their mothers or fathers are. Hundreds of thousands of children travel to prisons to visit their mothers, fathers, brothers and sisters every week. Leaders and lawmakers today should consider all these laws they are passing to lock people up, because when an individual is sent to prison, sometimes it affects an entire family. Yes, I agree some people need to be locked up. But, I also advocate for nonviolent drug addicts and first-time offenders who have not committed murder, rape, or crimes against the elderly or children, to be sentenced to some type of community-based program involving treatment and rehabilitation.

With this approach, the escalating violence being perpetrated by the youth today may be deterred. The sheer number of youths being adjudicated as adults and subjected to adult sentences is staggering, and the age of some of these offenders are as young as thirteen and fourteen. If this matter were scrutinized in conjunction with the alarming rate of recidivism, it would be clear these kids being placed in adult prisons are only creating younger and more violent criminals. At present, it may not seem significant, but these kids are the future. As more kids get involved in crime, fewer of them will have the rights to change the policies governing them.

There are two ways to change government and laws; through voting or seeking office. Both of these ways are nullified if someone is convicted of a felony because the right to vote is revoked and a former convict cannot serve as a public official or work in any capacity of local, state, or federal government, or at least most offices of government.

Something is causing these kids to be this way. If that cause continues to go unchecked, we could be the next victims by having one of these kids confront us and not only want to take our valuables, but they may not care about taking our lives. Without more options, the level of violence will inevitably increase. Without proper leadership, America will become stagnated and entrapped by its own devices.

CHAPTER 9

Opportunities

---◆---

The opportunities that exist in this country make people consider us the greatest country in the world. But, liberating every other country in the world seems more important than rescuing its own citizens from losing their homes and cars. Fulfilling goals and dreams are all but gone now. America seems to be more interested in savings than in hope in the American dream. Millions of Americans have lost their homes and not just the ones caught up in the housing crisis that began in 2007, but also the ones who had their homes for ten to fifteen years. Their home value declined and all of the equity they had accumulated vanished. America decided to use taxpayers' money to rescue the banks that collapsed during this time instead of helping the homeowners.

A question no one seems to have asked is if millions of Americans were duped into putting up what amounted to their entire savings, for some to close on millions of homes. If the banks didn't receive some of the proceeds, where did all the billions of dollars go? And why aren't there federal indictments charging those responsible for one or more of the many legal drugs such as alcohol or pain pills? Isn't it ironic that the three things killing more people in this country; alcohol, guns and tobacco, are all legal? The alternative to treatment, unless you are a celebrity of course, has become prison. I know I've mentioned it before, but I want to make sure those reading this book are aware of the number of people incarcerated in this country. These people, while in prison, have access to all the things hardworking Americans are struggling to have or keep. For example, 95 percent of all federal prisons have central air and heat, all the housing units have multiple televisions and some even have flat screens, all with cable channels. All have hot showers, and inmates are fed three hot meals a day. Their clothes are washed. They have access to e-mail on the internet. Their medical and dental appointments are only two dollars per visit, and if it's a follow-up, it's free. These are just a few things federal inmates have access to and some can make up to hundreds of dollars a month for working in factories.

These amenities are present for inmates not only in federal prison, but some of the same things if not more, are granted to state inmates as well. People who work hard are paying for this with taxpayers' money while they struggle for healthcare or to keep their lights from being shut off, which is how they get hot water, air conditioning, heat, television, cable and even internet access.

If we look at this situation objectively, we may conclude that a lot of the very things Americans are struggling to keep are being given to prisoners for free. All this is being done while every statistic and study suggests that rehab and alternatives to prison are the most effective ways to combat recidivism, and it's also more cost effective.

The opportunities for our youth have also diminished in regards to the jobs they once held during the summer while they were out of school. Older individuals are now taking those jobs because of the unemployment crisis. As these kids graduate from high school, some are faced with the reality they cannot afford college and there are no jobs available. The thing a lot of them have turned to is the military, which not only houses them; it also gives them a salary and a promise to pay their college expenses during their service. The only problem with that is so many of them are coming home mentally and physically disabled.

The leaders of this country must put forth a concerted effort to preserve the opportunities that allowed them to pursue their dreams for this generation of youth to pursue theirs. As opportunities decrease, so does the ambition to pursue dreams. With the death of dreams, the desire to fulfill one's destiny also dies. This is something our leaders do not need to put on the backburner while it tries to solve every other country's problem and try to be the world's police. These youth being treated as if they are expendable are the ones who will be in charge of the order and security of this country one day. It's obvious that today's leaders do not care about the opportunities simply based on the national debt being piled up that will end up being the kids of today problem of tomorrow.

I can't help but wonder if this all a part of a bigger picture when I think about how much more money is being spent on prisons than education. What will the picture show when all the pieces are put together? Will it be the one our leaders of America want us to see? How can the picture be clear considering the job situations, cars, homes, savings and good credit, which is what qualified us for all those things, are being lost? Add the national deficit and the astronomical number of people in prisons, the demise of the family, the number of incurable diseases, and the violence being perpetrated by our youth and the only picture I see is one of death and destruction.

The original forefathers of this country had in mind for things getting better for the generations to come and for dreams and opportunities being easier for us than it was for them. They also put the structure of the family as being the key element of democracy.

Now it seems that every president America elects, their first objective is to bomb the Middle East while professing to be liberating them. Every president, from Ronald Reagan and some before have conflicted with the Middle East. Reagan bombed them for eight years; then Bush Senior did it for four years; Clinton for eight more years, followed by Bush Junior for eight more years. As I'm writing this book, the current president is President Obama and he followed suit after Bush Junior, keeping troops in at least three regions of the Middle East for at least six years. Maybe it's time for America to refocus its priorities and put perspective on family values and opportunities for Americans rather than trying to ensure every other country has democracy.

I think one of the main reasons America will self-destruct is because of its love and fixation on riches and wealth. Americans have reached the point in their pursuit of riches where they will allow the same people from the countries they are at war with to become citizens. It's like straddling the fence saying although we're at war, only some of them are our enemies. America cannot continue to use a double-edged sword to fight its declared enemies. Using this approach can cut from either end it's handled from.

Without opportunities, this country is no different from than any other country. Opportunities are what makes America so appealing in the first place, so it's essential that they remain for this generation and its own citizens first.

CHAPTER 10

Care

To rectify some or all of the issues I've addressed, there must be a certain level of care. A lack of care is one of the contributing factors of how our bonds were broken. But with a renewed sense of care and concern, I believe most of our bonds can be restored.

Parents need to care about how they interact with their own parents, as well as their children. People need to care about respect and giving it as well as receiving it. People need to care about unity in their families as well as their communities. People also need to care about who's leading this country and where they are leading us. People should also care about the opportunities available before we realize there are none left. People should care about how many people are in prison. Why? Because we're paying for them to be there. Above all, everyone should care about God, a higher power, Allah, Jehovah, or believe in something relating to a religion or faith.

If the founding fathers of America did not care about its citizens, they never would have established a constitution declaring all men to have been created equal. With what was going on during the time and before the Emancipation Proclamation was written, it took not only care but also courage from those who wrote it. If things did not start with them caring, Martin Luther King Jr.'s dream probably would not have even become a thought. The initial care they displayed shows the potential a little care can have by looking at the progress that's been made when opportunities were available for all people. Care got it all started, and consideration has ushered opportunities to the point that two of the highest offices in government were held by African Americans: President of the United States of America and the office of the United States Attorney General.

The great pioneers of the Civil Rights Movement also cared about us to the point that some were willing to lay down their lives so we could have opportunities to be treated equally and be acknowledged as such. It seems only right that we acknowledge their sacrifices by caring about the very things they fought for, especially the respect of not being called niggers.

How black people today are so receptive to being called niggers by each other. Someone needs to show this generation the photos and film footage of the dog attacks, high-powered water hoses, beatings, and lynchings black people endured so they wouldn't be called niggers. Thank goodness they cared, as did others, or else I wouldn't have written this book. I wouldn't have known how because at one time so-called niggers weren't allowed to read.

I also want to touch on showing more care for women, especially from men who have children with women they have no contact with. Credit needs to be given to these women who have to play the role of both mother and father. I think it's safe to say most men love their mothers, which is why I find it hard to understand why they would not at least care about the mother of their own children. Something I have never understood and I'm sure I never will, is how a man can know he has a son and see the kid looks just like him and still not want to be involved in his life. How can a man do that to his little man?

Even if men don't care for the sacrifices being made by women, at least show some respect for them. If we go to the little league practice for football, soccer, or baseball, all we see are women. Women take care of getting our kids to school, the doctors and some even to church. They don't miss birthdays or holidays; they not only protect children, they also provide for them.

The executives of the large music companies need to start caring more about the negative influences the music they are producing is having on the youth of today rather than how much money they are making off it. This generation is influenced by music and the things the artists are singing about including sex and violence. The reason I say the music producers and executives need to care is because they listen to and approve these songs long before they reach us. They go along with producing and promoting the songs, even if it promotes violence, sex and using drugs. Not to mention, the dozen or so endorsements from almost every brand of alcohol and how drunk it will get one.

The CEO's in broadcasting need to also care more about how the shows and the violence and sex depicted in them are influencing the youth. It seems all they care about are ratings, which means money. It used to be a time when we could only see sex being portrayed on cable television, but now it's on basic TV as well. Almost every show is about murders, rapes, drugs, alcohol, violence and in a way they glorify crime. This also includes movies in theaters. A lot of the violence being portrayed by kids today is a result of it being seen and heard by them constantly through music and television programming.

The level of care needed also needs to extend to the makers of video games. At first, these games were for entertainment and enjoyment to show how technology has advanced. When I was a kid, the games were Pacman, Centipede and games like that. Now it's all about robbing, grand theft and graphically violent murders. It does not take a rocket scientist to figure out this stuff is influencing these children. Music, movies and video games are all about drugs, sex and violence. So if these executives don't care because of their greed, the leaders of Congress need to step up and start regulating these industries.

The truth is, we all need to care a little more not only about ourselves and our families, but also about our fellow citizens, communities, and country as a whole.

CHAPTER 11

Health

Health is another link that's missing from our society. I believe this is one of the sickest countries in the world if not, the sickest. By sickest, I mean its citizens are suffering. Prescription medications are one of the biggest and fastest growing industries, not only in this country but in the world. There seems to be a pill for everything we can imagine. It's even gotten to the point that people are getting prescriptions filled for their pets being diagnosed with symptoms of depression and even anxiety.

Regardless of what we go to a doctor for, it seems we will come out with a prescription. It's like if we tell them our backs hurt, we will get something for depression, along with some type of pain pill for our backs. If we tell a doctor we've had stress because of being behind on a few bills, a lot of doctors will say we may be depressed, even if we explain to them the stress only occurs and lasts until we get caught up on the bills.

While some of the medicine being prescribed may be necessary to treat some of the ailments people have today, most of the problems can probably be treated with proper diets and nutrition, especially with children. Some of these children are on more medication than their grandparents. So many are on medication for things that were just a part of growing up when I was young. Sure, some kids I grew up with and went to school with had problems. But it wasn't to the extreme where they had to be put on medication for the rest of their lives. As a matter of fact, all this stuff they are giving kids nowadays wasn't available to give them.

A lot of children are dependent on these medications they have been taking since they were barely past being toddlers. The statistics are staggering as to the number of children being treated for Attention Deficit/Hyperactivity Disorder, or ADHD. I wonder why people take their children to doctors and when they're told their children suffer from ADHD, they feel like the answer to the problem is to prescribe medicine that will sedate the children to the point of being inactive?

First of all, parents should give their children more attention to alleviate the deficit they suffer from. If I break down the words attention deficit disorder, attention is defined as notice or observation, also care or consideration. Deficit is described as meaning to lack, and disorder is defined as a lack of order and also to upset the normal functions of something or someone. I thought all parents paid attention to their kids and noticed and observed any changes in their physical appearance and overall state of mind.

When someone says it's some type of deficit, the way to alleviate it is to make up for whatever it is that's lacking. To go back to normal, people need to make time for their children and give them the attention they need to function normally. As I mentioned in the chapter on maturity, most of these kids only interact with their parents a few hours a day. How can these kids get attention from their parents, when a lot of their fathers are not involved in their lives and the mothers are at work all day, while the children are in school or some after-school program most of the day? This may be a contributing factor to a lot of deficits and disorders. Even when these kids get picked up from daycare, or wherever some of them are until their parents get off from work, or even if they are home alone until their parents get home, it's still limited interactions. By the time they eat dinner, it's time for a bath and bed shortly after.

This can also be draining for parents who have worked all day and have to come home to cook, deal with the kids, shower, and get ready for bed themselves. To me, this is why women deserve so much respect. Most often, it's women playing many different roles in and out of the home.

Considering the schedules of some parents, in relation to their children's schedules because of the conflicts of time, a child may act out for attention. That may not mean it's something wrong with the child. It may be the child just needs to be given some undivided attention.

When it comes to a lot of these illnesses children are being diagnosed with today and the epidemic of obesity amongst them, it all started with the generation of so-called "latch key kids." This was when kids had their house keys hanging from their necks, and they were expected to go straight home from school and call their parents as soon as they got there. They were told to call at certain times, or they received calls at certain times from their parents. The number-one rule was: do not open the door for anybody for any reason, even if it was God coming to take them to heaven! There was always microwaveable food so kids would not have to touch the stove, and snacks were abundant.

A lot of times, the parents would pick up fast food on the way home thinking it would take too long to cook a meal. As this continued, less and less time was spent at the dinner table which was when a lot of families discussed the day's events and personal thoughts.

As a result of this lifestyle, these kids started gaining weight from fast foods, sitting and lying around most of the time, eating snacks after school. Also contributing to this lifestyle was the evolution of video games. Kids nowadays find more entertainment in electronics than in physical exercise. The bottom line is kids don't go outside and play anymore. This not only affected the children's weight, but the parents' weights have also reached the point of obesity.

I look at my body and the human body in general, as a powerful machine. If one part is not working, it affects the whole body mentally, physically, emotionally as well as spiritually. They all have to be in tune for them to work at their full potential.

So, if someone is mentally lucid but morbidly obese, although they can function physically, it does not mean they are doing so at 100 percent. I'll compare it to a car that has a bad starter but a good engine. It will work sometimes, but it will eventually stop completely. Some people live their lives this way. They know there's a problem with their weight or something else, but they keep going until they have a heart attack or stroke. Being an adult, I understand in this life it's not about how fast we go, but rather how far we get that matters. We should not live our lives just to get by; we should be driven to get ahead.

As parents, we have to lead by example. This includes how and what we eat, exercising and staying in reasonable shape. This can be done by exercising a few times a week for thirty to forty-five minutes a day. The first fifteen minutes can be for stretching, which is a great exercise. This time can also be used to discuss the day's events. The remaining time can be used to do cardio, sit-ups, jumping jacks, jump rope, running in place, walking on the treadmill, doing squats, leg raises, knee lifts, or any exercise for at least thirty minutes. This time will pass quickly and it will be stimulating and energizing. As one gets more into it, one can increase the time exercising which will also increase the benefits of doing so.

Getting in shape will get rid of some of the physical, mental, and emotional ailments so many people are suffering from. Being in good health also creates self-awareness, and I think it's necessary to inspire people to practice safe sex. Sex today is like playing Russian roulette with four bullets in a five-chambered gun. More diseases are facing this generation than any other before. AIDS, HIV, and numerous other sexually transmitted diseases cannot only alter our health, they can also kill us. So it's imperative we protect our health from preventable diseases.

CHAPTER 12

Prisons

T hroughout this book, I have made references to prisons being the cause of several links being broken. This chapter is to put my reasons for feeling this way forthright. By doing so, I hope it will shed light on this subject, as well as scrutiny.

Again, let me start by saying America has more people in prisons than any other country in the world. I want to reiterate there are 1.5 million in prisons and hundreds of thousands in jails, with many of those facing the possibility of being sentenced to prison.

The numbers are disproportionate to say the least, especially considering China has a population of over 2 billion people. But it's nowhere near the number of people in prison as America that boasts a population of only 330 million citizens.

In Chapter 9 titled Opportunities, I wrote about some of the amenities in prison. In this chapter however, I will point out the inhumane treatment and conditions prisoners are faced with. First and foremost, to be incarcerated period is degrading and in a lot of prisons, it can be extremely dangerous.

Prison was designed for people considered a danger to society. But today, it seems like it's strictly business. There are millionaires investing millions of dollars into private prisons. Their primary purpose is to warehouse bodies for profit.

When a person is sentenced to these prisons, the prisoner is subjected to sleeping in dormitories with 150 to 200 inmates. One person may have anywhere from one to five years, while the person sleeping next to him may have 50 or even a hundred years and a hundred years is not an exaggerated sentence for some prisoners. Likewise, one person could have been sent to prison for a drug-related offense and ended up sleeping next to a serial killer.

Most prison systems have what's called high, medium and low-security institutions supposedly to prevent these types of housing problems. But it all comes down to where there is a bed available.

In these type of environments, you can see violent things as well as disgusting situations. Homosexual behavior is common in prisons. Although I agree people have the right to choose their sexual orientation in prisons, it's more force or should I say deception used with those involved in gay relationships than it simply being a choice. The reason I say force and deception is because most gay individuals are educated law-abiding citizens who rarely, if ever, get incarcerated. Yet the number of people involved in homosexual relationships in prison can be the majority of the compound in one way or another. This shows a lot of people are becoming gay after going to prison. Inmates with life-threatening diseases are not segregated from the rest of the prison. An inmate with syphilis or HIV positive is housed with the general population. Since they are sexually transmitted diseases, the prison staff doesn't feel like anyone is at risk because sexual contact is against the rules in all prison systems. They access the risk as being zero if a person doesn't get involved in homosexual activity.

The problem with this approach is, despite the rules, sexual activity is constant between inmates and so is the number of sexually transmitted diseases being carried back into society and transmitted with impunity. A lot of the people who have contracted these diseases don't know they are infected. Believe it or not, a lot don't want to know if they have been exposed. When they are released from prison, they inject themselves back into the dating pool.

I've already stated the average relationship lasts only three to six months. By the time people realize they're sick, they could have been in and out of several relationships and in the process exposed or infected several people. I would not consider it an overstatement to say that prisons are breeding grounds for diseases to be transmitted. In turn, these infected people are released from prison and go on to infect even more people. In light of this deadly chain of events, it happens daily across America and will continue at an accelerated pace without intervention and prevention.

Another thing that's happening in prisons being played out in society is violence. In prison, the level of violence can reach the point of death. Some prisons are strictly gang-related and everything revolves around gang rules and mentalities. In some prisons, gangs considered mortal enemies are housed in the same area. When this happens, it's inevitable that violence will occur. Yet, this too is evident in prisons across America. This could set into motion the scenario of one inmate with a short sentence being housed with those with life sentences or nonviolent inmates. The one with the short sentence can be enticed to be violent or risk becoming a victim of violence. So a person who may have been a drug offender can easily become extremely violent. When normal people are exposed to constant violence, they become potentially violent themselves. These are the same people who will eventually end up back in society.

If someone wonders if the violence inmates are exposed to in prison is carried out by some who are released back into society, all one needs to do is look at the recidivism. It shows how most inmates who return to prison have their crimes progress in the direction of violence. If this is accepted as being the truth, then there are two potentially dangerous ways inmates are being released back into society. One is being exposed to sexually transmitted diseases that could be spread in society and two those who will have an inherent penchant to commit violence.

Some may wonder how these two subjects factor in this book. To that I will say, the diseases being spread coincides with the chapter of health and violence does likewise with the chapters of respect and care. With violence, we can be certain there will be no respect and disregard for caring.

Incarceration also affects families and their structure. Most people locked up have families, which may include parents, kids, siblings, a girlfriend/boyfriend, wife, or husband. The impact on these relationships can be devastating and cause irreversible damage to the bonds that once held them together.

The relationships of fathers and sons being separated are the ones having the most evident impact on society. This is not to say children are not being impacted by the loss of their mothers. However, it is evident there are substantially more men in prison than women and likewise the juvenile offenders are significantly more males than females.

In my opinion, this is the result of several factors: The content of music greatly influencing our youth, the violence, sex and drug use on TV programs, movies, peer pressure along with being raised by young single mothers, who may not be as mature as needed to assume the role of both mother and father, figuratively speaking. Even a single mother with her morals, principals, and values up to par and does for her son, the child can still end up taking the wrong path because he has no father figure in his life to humble him.

In a lot of homes, mothers have moved on to other relationships that will give the children a stepfather. But, regardless of their intent or involvement, these kids may accept them as taking their father's space, but they still won't be able to take their birth father's place.

I mentioned in an earlier chapter these kids are bigger than normal. It doesn't take much to set these kids off when they see and hear violence on TV and in music every day, all day. Then to know one or both of their parents are in prison can influence them to act out. The chance of them acting out is increased when the kid does something and the other parent makes statements that they're just like their mother or father and is headed to the same place. One thing that can cause some of these boys to act out is the stepfathers. In some cases, they can look at a kid who is not theirs as being bad, and they do everything they can to make it uncomfortable for the child until he would rather be locked up than to live there because the child already feels like he is living in hell.

More times than not, many women are desperate to keep a man for companionship or that in conjunction with financial help and will not intervene to protect their child from what could amount to psychological, emotional, or even physical abuse. Some kids may take this as her choosing him over them and shut down on caring about anything. The sad part about this is the one person who could probably turn the kid around is locked up miles away in some prison. When this happens, most of the time the mother has closed all lines of communications between the child, his father and the father's family.

I say it again; these kids will seek out their fathers when they become the age where they start to venture out on their own. When they meet them, all it will take is for the fathers to say, "I love you" and the children will embrace them. It won't be about the money the mothers complained about not getting throughout the years. To the children, it will only be about being acknowledged and accepted by their fathers.

Prisons are one of the causes and effects of these events being put into motion. This is especially true of the cases where the children grow up with fathers, only to have them taken away at young ages for years or even forever! I do agree some people need to be locked up in prison. But prisons are filled with people who may be drug addicts or petty criminals, who should be in treatment centers rather than prisons.

Prisons are becoming more about employment than rehabilitation and taxpayers are the ones paying for all of it. The amount of money being spent on prisons surpasses the entire amount being spent on the educational system. This includes colleges, universities and public schools combined.

While lawmakers have told the public it's all about safety, in truth, it's only about being reelected when it comes to their stances on crime. The problem with this is politicians think this Ronald Reagan approach is still what the public wants. But society is not being fully informed about how they will be the ones paying for it.

This is the primary reason I included prisons as being an area that bonds are being broken. It's draining society of money and resources; it's breeding violent and more dangerous criminals. Prisons are destroying families and the relationships between parents and children. Prisons are also infested with diseases that are being spread in society by people being released.

To conclude this chapter, I want to say that in my opinion, prisons are counterproductive and detrimental to the family structure as well as society. Prisons are the devil's playgrounds and will remain that way until efforts are restored to rehabilitate inmates rather than warehousing them for jobs and money from private investors.

The revolving doors holding these prisoners in will be the same ones that will eventually swing open to let them back out. When most of these guys get out, they're bigger, stronger and some are more dangerous than they were before. Some will have the mentality that society has victimized them and it will be time for society to pay the piper.

CHAPTER 13

A Higher Power "God"

Faith answers questions rather than cause them to be asked. Through faith, I believe God knows everything we go through. I've evolved to the point in my life where I don't question His will or His way. Nor do I complain. His grace is sufficient to sustain me beyond all doubt. As the book of Romans 8:38-39, says, "For I am convinced that neither death nor life, neither angels nor demons, neither the present or the future, nor any powers, neither height nor depth, nor anything else in all creation will be able to separate us from the love of God that is in Jesus."

Before I go any further, I want to acknowledge I was brought up in a Baptist church. I accept this teaching as being the truth. I also believe Islam, the Catholic religion and all other beliefs involving a higher power are all part of the truth.

Being a man, I don't necessarily need someone to influence me about what is or isn't true. I on my own know the truth is unwavering and cannot be compromised. My acceptance of these truths involving it being a God has convinced me to believe God is the most important link to keep us connected to love and our families. I came to the knowledge of this truth when I grew to believe all things are possible through faith. When I say all things are possible, I mean that. I have been in some situations in my life that there was no way I emerged to the other side of them without having some type of divine intervention.

I also believe in God, based on an event involving my stepfather, who was in the hospital with full-blown AIDS. My niece was graduating from high school in Atlanta, Georgia and my stepfather, whose name was Sam, had taken a turn for the worst. According to his doctor, he was in his final days.

My mother wanted desperately to be at the graduation, but had a dilemma. She reconsidered leaving Sam, thinking he would pass before she made it back. After repeatedly assuring her everything would be okay, she decided to go to graduation. My sister Shelia drove my Mother to Atlanta. About the time they arrived there, I remember receiving a call from Sam's daughter, Angie. She was screaming at the top of her lungs, saying the hospital had called to say Sam had gone into *code blue*. In medical terms, code blue meant he could die and needed to be revived. I dropped the phone and began praying like never before. What I said, I will keep to myself, except to say I told God that for as long as I could remember, I've always heard that He would not put more on us than we can handle and if Sam died while my mom was in Atlanta, it would be too much for her.

When I finished saying some other things and came out of the spirit, I realized I had left Angie on the phone. At the time, I was not aware of how long I had been praying. I was in a realm I cannot explain, except to say I was in "the spirit."

I realized Angie was no longer on the phone, so I hung up and called her back. Before I could finish, she was calling back to say the hospital had called back to say Sam had somehow stabilized again and all his vital signs were back to normal. Angie said she thought she heard me talking to someone else, so she hung up. I told her I was praying and he would be fine. Sam stayed stable for the next few days, and my mom returned on the day expected. She went to the hospital the next morning and soon after her arrival, Sam went back into code blue and passed with my mother at his side along with my sister, who had become her constant and faithful companion.

I was thankful to God my mom got to be with Sam and at the same time I knew God was real and His words were true, especially when He said He would never leave us nor forsake us. I have had many other times in my life since then that has affirmed He is always with me.

I want to paint a picture of how I became involved with pursuing if there was a God to me. I love science and astrology. I've always been fascinated by images taken by the Hubble Telescope. In these photographs, we can see other galaxies, solar systems and images of things that seem divine to me. What we can't see though is there are photos of these places considered light years away, in which one light year is approximately 5.9 trillion miles away. So traveling at the speed of light, we would have to travel 5.9 trillion miles to get there. And some of the Hubble's photos depict places thousands of light years away. We can't see any other life-sustaining planets. Nothing is living within our solar system or any other that man has discovered. Not one place within untold trillions of miles of Earth even has air and there's a debate about the possibility of water being found. As far as we know there is no other life anywhere, not even a plant. From this, I am convinced it's more than a coincidence that Earth has all the elements needed to sustain life in one place. The only place we happen to be. To me, this does not require a lot of debate or questioning. I came up with the word faithscience to describe that through faith, I believe there's a God. It's also my belief that science and nature cannot refute this. If anything, it affirms that divine influence created the universe and everything in it, including us.

In understanding how or why I believe in God, I have to explain why I believe God is essential to restoring the bonds that have been broken. It's like the further we as people moved away from God, the further we went from having a conscience to not caring about our families, not respecting each other, love, relationships, unity and even ourselves.

The more man tries to fix things, the worse things seem to get. When we try to fix something, it's from and according to our own understanding and for the benefit of serving ourselves.

When God fixes something, it's according to His infinite wisdom which exceedingly surpasses our own wisdom and understanding. He does it for His glory to be seen and He fixes it so it won't need to be repaired again. Nowadays when we talk to people in distress about turning to God to get Him to resolve whatever problem they may have, people get offensive or downright disrespectful and tell us flat out they don't want to hear anything about God or about praying to Him. These people are convinced everything bad they go through is because God let it happen. But when something good happens to them, they think it's good luck, or they made it happen.

When things seem to be totally out of control and as bad as they can be, that's when God is at His best. It's at these times that He can show how He can make it better than it ever was. The book of Job is a great example of this. Job lost everything and everyone around him. But through his faith, he endured the trials. In the end, Job had twice the amount of everything he had before his troubles began. If studied, it can be said that all of the saints went through hard times. Jesus was beaten, spit on and even crucified. John the Baptist was beheaded. Paul described in 2 Corinthians the things he endured. In 2 Corinthians 11:23-27 Paul says, "I have worked much harder, been in prison more frequently, been flogged more severely and been exposed to death again forty lashes minus one. Three times I was beaten with rods; once I was stoned; three times I was shipwrecked; I spent a night and a day in the open sea. I have been constantly on the move. I have been in danger from rivers, in danger from bandits, in danger from my own countrymen, in danger from Gentiles, in danger in the city, in danger in the country, in danger at sea, and in danger from false brothers. I have labored and toiled and have often gone without sleep; I have known hunger and thirst and have often gone without food. I have been cold and naked." Paul endured all this and in the end, Chapter 12:9, Paul says that he will boast all the more gladly about his weaknesses, so that Christ's power may rest on him. Verse 10 says, "That is why, for Christ's sake, I delight in weaknesses, in insults, in hardships, in persecutions, in difficulties, for when I am weak, then am I strong."

The difference between these saints and people today is that they never stopped believing and people today never started. People will let trivial things stop them from acknowledging God when all they need to do is believe that with God, all things are possible. Matthew 6:5-13 teaches us how to pray and tells us it's not a lot of words that are the right way or in front of people, but rather in private. Like Chapter 6:8 says, "For your father knows what you need before you ask Him."

If nothing else, if people would adhere to Matthew 7:7-12, the majority of the problems we're dealing with would rectify themselves. Verse 7 starts by saying, "Ask and it will be given to you, seek and you will find; knock and the door will be opened to you. For everyone who asks receives; he who seeks finds; and to him who knocks, the door will be opened."

Verse 9 goes on and asks the question, "Which of you if his son asks for bread, will give him a stone? Or if he asks for a fish, will give him a snake? If you, then, though are a sinner, know how to give good gifts to your children, how much more will your Father in heaven give good gifts to those who ask him?" Verse 12 says, "So in everything, do to others what you would have them to do to you, for this sums up the law and the prophets."

This is something we should all start to do, to treat each other the way we would want people to treat us. We can get started by first giving credence to the word of God and acknowledging that they are truly His words and His will for us to follow them.

Regardless of who or what we choose to call God, as long as we believe, we are doing the most important thing we can in relation to faith, which is nothing more than believing.

In the book of James, Chapter 2, he describes how faith comes with works. They are the things we do accordingly to the Scriptures to show we believe in the Word. And even though someone may claim to have faith, they give no examples of it by demonstrating charity, compassion, endurance, or ministering. By the lack of these things, it shows they don't have faith at all. James sums it up in Chapter 2:14-19 by saying, "What good is it, my brothers, if a man claims to have faith but have no deeds? Can such a faith save him? Suppose a brother or sister is without clothes and daily food. If one of you says to him, 'Go, I wish you well; keep warm and well fed,' but does nothing about his physical needs, what good is it? In the same way, faith by itself, if it is not accompanied by action, is dead."

But someone will say, "You have faith; I have deeds. Show me your faith without deeds, and I will show you my faith by what I do. You believe that there is one God. Good! Even the demons believe that and tremble."

As the leaders of our children, we must put these kids in touch with religion so they will stand for something and stop falling for anything. As adults, we need to go back to our roots that were instilled in us as children by our grandparents. To those who did not have this in their upbringing, they need to come to the knowledge of the truth that God is the way, the truth and the light that can illuminate the darkest moments of any night.

Once we become adults, we must give an account for ourselves and be responsible for our own destinies. Being an adult has nothing to do with age. It's our mentalities that measure our level of maturity. As Paul says in 1 Corinthians, Chapter 13:11, "When I was a child, I talked like a child. I thought like a child. I reasoned like a child. When I became a man, I put childish ways behind me."

Act your age and realize these children are following our lead. If as an adult, you have chosen not to believe in God, that's your decisions. But at least point your children in that direction to let them make that choice for themselves. When I say point them in that direction, I mean don't discourage them.

Anything positive we can put in these kids' lives is better than all the negative stuff they are being influenced by today.

Conclusion

Throughout history, every great empire has come to an end by one means or another. America is on the road to becoming the next great country that will fall victim to this statistic. How this will happen will be an implosion. The main cause of this will be the total devastation of middle-class America. As with everything, if we take the middle out of something, the top is going to fall on the bottom. While this is happening across America, it's creating two distinct groups; rich being one and poor being the other. If America does not categorically address the issues causing the systematic breakdown of families, communities and the democracy that made it the most liberated country in the world, there will be a continued decline in morals, principles and values among its citizens.

The topics I chose for this book are just some of the problems we are facing. Chapter one addressed the subject of love and relationships. To add to that, I feel we should first love ourselves and any relationship we get involved in should serve as an enhancer to our own, which is the foundation that upholds firmly in place our beliefs of principals above pleasure. If we begin to discern the distinct differences between love and lust, we will save ourselves a lot of pain. It may even save our lives considering the amount of sexually transmitted diseases in the world today. Being in lust can lead us to get involved in a relationship with someone who may have been involved with someone who may have been involved with five other people and each one of those five people may have been involved with five other people and each of those with five others. While five is a conservative number, the point is we can be in lust with one person and be exposed to hundreds or even thousands of different people's DNAs. In simple terms, when we have sex with one person, we are having sex with everyone they've had sex with and the people they've had sex with and it goes on and on. It's like playing Russian roulette. If there are five chambers in a gun and one has a bullet in it, if we keep pulling the trigger, it will eventually fire a bullet. Having unprotected sex is just as dangerous as playing Russian roulette. They both could potentially kill us with the first chance we take.

Chapter two was about the love of money being the root of all evil. On any given day, we can turn on the news and hear about some of the atrocious things people are doing in their pursuit of money or how their lack of having it drove them to the point of murder to get it. I've concluded that slow money is show money and fast money don't last.

Chapter three touched on maturity. When reached, it causes us to give accountability of ourselves and guides us to become more discreet in our choices. With maturity, we care about what we do and how it affects others. It gives us better relationship qualities and respect becomes our motto.

Chapter four on respect was a subject I tried approaching with the sacrifices of the great civil rights pioneers in mind. I wanted to shed light on the things they endured, encountered and overcame so the youth of today would have freedom to pursue stability in love, life, health and wealth. Although we have come ninety-nine miles, we still have one to go! One thing we cannot do to slow ourselves down is to call ourselves the very names our elders fought and faced death so we wouldn't be called anything less than men and women. I wish I could get every one of these kids today to see some of the things blacks went through to not be called niggers only to have them stand in front of white people and call each other niggers. All I can say is God forgive them for they know not what they do.

Chapter five spoke on unity, which is what's needed to guide this generation back to the straight and narrow. Even though these are not our children and we may not be related to them, we are still their elders. We are responsible for leading them the right way, just as our elders did for us.

Chapter six mentioned fathers being one of the missing links. Fathers are the first men in their children's lives, so it's important these kids have relationships with them. Fathers can also be the glue to keeping families together and likewise humble young men, who are becoming more and more out of control. The young men who have found themselves being given the title of father, need to realize they have children. So for them to continue to act like children is not acceptable. To the fathers who have little men who are the spitting image of them, how can you, as human beings, deny your own sons? It does not matter what the circumstances were as far as how he was conceived whether the relationship was serious, casual, or a one-night stand. Regardless if the feelings for the mothers were filled with malice, that still should not be an excuse for not being involved in your children's lives, especially men who were raised without their father in their lives and the effect it had in their lives. Your children are your blessings and don't deserve to be treated like burdens.

I intentionally made chapter seven based on families and their importance. It is the middle of this book. To me, this is the most important part because it covers the bottom, while at the same time, it upholds the top. This country is distinguished by democracy and the structure of the family is the foundation of where the principals of democracy are first learned. Families are also where we learn about love, respect, unity, leadership, care and about God. If we come from close-knit families, we will easily adapt to the family of society. In every family, there is someone respected by everyone else in the family. Whether this is a male or a female, they have to become the leader of the family and rally the family together for functions and gatherings. They need to set a standard that must be met but not exceeded for everyone to follow. They must lead by example!

Chapter eight addressed the very subject of leadership. The leaders of today are so obsessed with their own successes and material gains; they are more like running away from the people rather than leading them. It's to the point that the so-called leaders need to be led themselves. Dr. Martin Luther King Jr. and John F. Kennedy were great leaders. They inspired the entire nation to change for the betterment of the world. Although what they did was in the United States, it had far reaching implications that transcended languages and racial boundaries. In politics, it all comes down to Republicans uniting with Republicans and Democrats are only aligning themselves with Democrats. They have all forgotten about the people who elected them and all stand with their arms outstretched and hands open for donations from every special interest group. Even the leaders of families once considered the matriarch or patriarch has all but disappeared. The main reason is because the youth do not respect the elders in their families. When there is a family get together, the grandparents see the way these kids act today and how hostile and disrespectful they are, so they don't interact with them. There was a time when families would get together for every holiday, birthday, or any special occasion and the grandparents would be treated like royalty. Nowadays, it seems like the only time the entire family gets together is for funerals. As parents, we need to restore our parents who are our children's grandparents, back to the place of being respected by every member of the family. The wisdom and values they have can be handed down to their youth.

Chapter nine confronted the problem concerning the lack of opportunities in America for its citizens to pursue their dreams and goals. With all the jobs continuing to be sent overseas, it's leaving behind a void as far as the people here being able to work to pursue their goals of being successful. Schools are raising tuition each year, so the dream of attending college is too expensive. And with the unemployment rate being as high as it is, where are the opportunities for us? They are all overseas with the jobs sent there. If the so-called leaders of Congress had placed a high tax penalty on businesses that sought employees from other countries so they could pay less in wages, they would be better off if they got people from America to do it. Maybe then, the economy in this country would not be in the shape it's in today. Someone in Congress, the White House, or from any one of the many unnecessary branches of government need to realize that for every dollar being sent overseas via jobs, it's probably equivalent to a thousand dollars being taken away from our own economy.

Chapter ten confronted care. I felt this was important to address because to mend most of the bonds that have been broken, we have to first care that they are. Care is always accompanied by consideration. With consideration, we think of how what we do will affect others before we do them—not after. Caring for young ladies is important. By caring, they will respect their bodies and the images they project. The book of Proverbs says in Chapter 11:22, "Like a jewel in a pig's nose, so is a beautiful woman who shows no discretion." What that's saying is even though some women are beautiful, some of the things they do still make them ugly. I've heard it said that some of the prettiest people do the ugliest things. Female strippers are a good example of this. But if someone loves money more than themselves, it does not matter.

Chapter eleven was on health. America is the sickest and most obese country in the world. Even our pets are on medication and overweight. So many electronics are entertaining the kids today until all they exercise are their fingers. They sit in school all day then go home and sit or lay down all night. While at home, they are either listening to some negative music or watching something on TV containing drugs, sex, or violence. If this trend continues, American youth will have more health problems than their grandparents. The best place for parents to start getting their kids in shape is to get themselves in shape as an example. Whether people realize it or not, parents are the first teachers of their children. More than anywhere, what these kids see at home will shape them into who they will become.

Chapter twelve must be considered when addressing some of the problems facing our country. To use its citizens as a means of employment is no better that what Castro, Hitler, or any other tyrant has done to its citizens. Prisons are directly responsible for the breakup of a lot of families; prisons also are turning men into monsters. Prisons are stripping people of all their senses and causing them to become callous. All they see for years are neutral colors. Their sense of smell is shut down. There is no contact with women. All they see are the same people, colors and place for years. The food is on a five-week cycle for years, which means when the menu gets to week five, it starts back over to week one again. And they are eating the same processed food for years. When these people are released, and a lot of them will be, they won't care about anything or anybody but themselves. They will have lost their families, friends and in some cases, their feelings for anything. With over 1.5 million men and women in prison, that's a lot society will have to deal with one day or every day because people are being released every day.

Chapter thirteen was my way of giving God the glory He deserves. When I began this book, I was reluctant to include a chapter on God. With it being so many different religions and beliefs, I didn't want to offend anyone about what their truth is. But I didn't write this book to offend people or teach them; I wrote it because these issues need to be addressed and mainly my concern that our youth society as well as their families are giving up on. I believe that if people start to inject God back into their families, it will make a profound difference in its unity and stability. My position is, as long as we acknowledge a higher power, we are doing what's right. Whatever we believe, try to let it include love, which covers a multitude of sins.

This book is only based on my observations. I feel we, as a country, need to address. Some may apply to you, and there may be issues I didn't bring up that's a problem or concern in your life. Regardless if they are my problems or yours, they need to be fixed because we all belong to the same family of society.

ACKNOWLEDGMENTS

I would like to acknowledge my advisor/consultant Mr. Eli Blyden. Thank you, Eli, for all your work on my books and getting all of them on the market and pushing them to get published.

Thank you for your patience and guidance to ensure I had the outcome I envisioned. Your willingness to go beyond the call of duty is equaled by your professionalism and persistence to attain perfection.

Thank you sir, your assistance was greatly appreciated and without you I would not have gotten where I'm at today with the books being completed. It is my true hope that our Lord will keep you and your family in His sight.

–Thank you, good brother, Shalom

www.ingramcontent.com/pod-product-compliance
Lightning Source LLC
Chambersburg PA
CBHW071618040426
42452CB00009B/1386